RISE AND GRIND

A Step-by-Step Guide to Building Your Dream Business from Scratch.

Robert J. Williams

DISCLAIMER

TABLE OF CONTENTS

INTRODUCTION

Do you have a business idea that you're passionate about but don't know where to start? Are you tired of feeling stuck in your current job and want to create a business that aligns with your values and goals? If so, this book is for you.

Rise and Grind is a step-by-step guide to building your dream business from scratch. In this book, you'll learn the strategies and techniques used by successful entrepreneurs to turn their ideas into profitable businesses. From finding your niche and developing a business plan, to marketing your product or service and managing your finances, this book covers all the essential steps to starting a business.

But more than just a practical guide, Rise and Grind is a book about mindset. It's about the discipline, resilience, and determination required to turn your dreams into reality. You'll learn how to overcome the obstacles that inevitably arise when starting a business, and how to cultivate the mindset of a successful entrepreneur.

Throughout this book, you'll hear from successful entrepreneurs who have been through the ups and downs of starting a business. They share their stories, insights, and practical tips for building a business that can thrive in today's competitive market.

Whether you're just starting out or looking to take your existing business to the next level, Rise and Grind is the ultimate guide to building a successful business. So let's get started and turn your dream into a reality!

CHAPTER ONE

"The Spark: Finding Your Passion and Ideation"

Starting a business is an exciting and challenging journey. Before you begin, it's important to first find your passion and identify your business idea. This will not only help you stay motivated throughout the journey, but it will also increase your chances of success.

Finding Your Passion

Finding your passion in business can be a challenging but rewarding journey. It is important to take the time to reflect on your strengths, interests, and values to understand what drives you and what you are truly passionate about. This can involve trying out new experiences, taking courses or workshops, and speaking to others who are successful in their careers.

Once you have a better understanding of your passions, it is crucial to align them with your career goals and find a way to incorporate them into your work. This can be as simple as finding a job that aligns with your passions or starting your own business that allows you to pursue your passions on a daily basis.

It is important to remember that finding your passion in business takes time and effort, and it may take several tries before you find the right fit. However, when you finally discover your passion, it can bring immense fulfillment and satisfaction to your work, leading to a successful and enjoyable career. So, never give up on your search and always be open to new opportunities and experiences that can help you find your passion in business.

In addition to reflection and exploration, it is also important to be proactive in seeking out opportunities that will help you find your passion in business. Networking events, trade shows, and industry conferences can provide exposure to different business fields and connect you with people who can offer advice and guidance. These experiences can also help you build relationships and gain valuable knowledge that can help you better understand what you are looking for in your career.

One of the benefits of finding your passion in business is that it can lead to increased motivation and productivity. When you are passionate about what you do, you are more likely to be engaged, focused, and dedicated to your work. This can translate into better performance and more opportunities for growth and advancement.

It is also important to maintain balance in your life as you pursue your passion in business. Burnout is a common challenge for many entrepreneurs and professionals, and it is essential to take care of your physical and mental well-being as you build your career. This can involve setting boundaries, taking breaks, and prioritizing self-care to ensure that you have the energy and motivation to pursue your passions in the long-term.

Finally, it is essential to stay open-minded and flexible in your pursuit of finding your passion in business. The business world is constantly changing, and you may find that your passions and interests shift over time. It is important to be willing to adapt and evolve, and to continuously seek out new experiences and opportunities that will help you grow and succeed in your career

Your passion is what drives you and motivates you to work hard. It's what you're most interested in and what you'd be willing to do for free. When you start a business based on your passion, it becomes more enjoyable and less like work. To find your passion, take some time to reflect on what you love to do. Ask yourself:

- What are you naturally good at?

- What do you enjoy doing in your free time?

- What causes or issues are you passionate about?

Once you've identified your passions, think about how you can turn them into a business idea. For example, if you love cooking, you could start a catering business. If you're passionate about environmental issues, you could start a green consulting firm.

Identifying Your Business Idea

Once you've found your passion, it's time to turn it into a business idea. Here are some steps to help you:

1.   Research the market: Research your industry and identify what products or services are currently being offered. Look for gaps in the market and think about how you can fill them.

2.   Identify your target audience: Who are you trying to serve? What are their needs and wants? Understanding

your target audience will help you tailor your business idea to their needs.

3.   Validate your idea: Talk to potential customers and ask for their feedback. This will help you determine whether there is a demand for your product or service and make any necessary adjustments.

4.   Get creative: Don't be afraid to think outside the box. Consider new and innovative ways to solve a problem or meet a need.

Remember, the key to a successful business is finding something you're passionate about and turning it into a viable business idea. This will help you stay motivated and focused throughout the journey.

In conclusion, finding your passion and ideation is the first step in starting a successful business. Take your time, do your research, and get creative. With the right idea and a lot of hard work, you can turn your dream into a reality.

Now, how do you possibly find your passion?

Finding your business passion can be a journey of self-discovery and exploration. Here are some steps you can follow to help you on your journey:

1. Reflect on your strengths, interests, and values: Take the time to consider what you are naturally good at, what you enjoy doing, and what is important to you. This

can give you insight into what you might be passionate about in a business context.

2. Try new things: Experiment with different business-related activities, such as volunteering, internships, or taking courses, to gain exposure to different industries and roles.

3. Network and gather information: Reach out to people in your network who are successful in their careers and seek their advice and guidance. Attend industry events and conferences to learn about different business fields and connect with others who have similar interests.

4. Align your passions with your career goals: Once you have a better understanding of your passions, it's important to consider how they align with your long-term

career goals. This can involve finding a job that aligns with your passions or starting your own business.

5.   Stay open-minded and flexible: Finding your business passion may take time and effort, and you may need to try different things before you find the right fit. It's important to stay open-minded and be willing to adapt and evolve as your passions and interests change.

6.   Prioritize balance: As you pursue your business passion, it's important to maintain a healthy work-life balance and take care of your physical and mental well-being.

By following these steps, you can find your business passion and build a successful and fulfilling career in the business world.

CHAPTER TWO

"Market Research: Understanding Your Target Audience"

Market research is an essential step in starting a business as it helps you validate your idea and understand your target audience. It's important to invest time and effort into market research to ensure that your business is solving a real problem and that there is a demand for your product or service.

Market research is a crucial step in starting a business as it helps you validate your idea and understand your target audience. The first step in market research is to define your target audience, which is the group of people you're trying to serve with your business. Understanding your target audience will allow you to tailor your business to their needs and create a product or service that they will love.

To define your target audience, consider their demographics such as age, gender, income, education, and more. Think about their interests and hobbies, their pain points, and what problems they need solving. Also, consider where they spend their time, whether it's online or in-person, to better understand how to reach them.

Once you've defined your target audience, the next step is to validate your business idea. This involves testing your idea to see if there is a demand for your product or service. You can validate your idea by conducting surveys or focus groups, researching your competitors, or launching a minimum viable product (MVP). These techniques will help you understand what potential customers like and dislike about your idea, as well as identify any gaps in the market that you can fill.

Finally, it's important to continually monitor and analyze your target audience and market to ensure that your business stays relevant and meets their evolving needs. This can be done through regular surveys, focus groups, and data analysis. By continually understanding your target audience and market, you can make informed decisions and improve your business over time.

In conclusion, market research is a critical component of starting a business. By defining your target audience, validating your business idea, and continually monitoring and analyzing your market, you can increase your chances of success and create a product or service that your target audience will love. Invest time and effort into market research to ensure the success of your business.

Defining Your Target Audience

The first step in market research is to define your target audience. Your target audience is the group of people you're trying to serve with your business. To define your target audience, you need to understand their needs, wants, and behaviors. Consider the following questions:

• Who are your potential customers?

• What are their demographics (age, gender, income, education, etc.)?

• What are their interests and hobbies?

• What are their pain points and what problems do they need solving?

• Where do they spend their time (online, in-person, etc.)?

By understanding your target audience, you can tailor your business to their needs and create a product or service that they will love.

Validating Your Business Idea

The next step in market research is to validate your business idea. This involves testing your idea to see if there is a demand for your product or service. There are a few ways to validate your idea, including:

1. Conducting surveys or focus groups: Ask potential customers for their opinions on your idea. This will help

you understand what they like and dislike about your idea and whether there is a demand for it.

2.   Competitor analysis: Research your competitors to see what they're offering and what makes them successful. This will help you understand the market and identify any gaps that you can fill.

3.   Launching a minimum viable product (MVP): An MVP is a basic version of your product or service that you can launch to test the market. This will help you validate your idea and make any necessary adjustments before launching a full version.

By conducting market research, you can ensure that your business idea is viable and that there is a demand for your product or service.

In conclusion, market research is an essential step in starting a business. By defining your target audience and validating your business idea, you can increase your chances of success and create a product or service that your target audience will love. Make sure to invest time and effort into market research to ensure the success of your business.

Collecting Data and Analyzing Your Results

Once you've defined your target audience and validated your business idea, it's time to collect data and analyze your results. There are a few ways to collect data, including:

1. Surveys and questionnaires: You can use online survey tools such as SurveyMonkey to send out surveys to your target audience. Ask questions about their needs, wants, and opinions on your business idea.

2. Focus groups: You can conduct focus groups to get a more in-depth understanding of your target audience. Gather a small group of people who represent your target audience and ask them questions about your business idea.

3. Online research: You can also use online tools such as Google Trends and Keyword Planner to research the demand for your business idea.

Once you've collected your data, it's important to analyze it to get insights into your target audience. Look for patterns and trends in the data and use it to inform your business decisions.

Market research is a vital step in starting a business as it provides several advantages in understanding your target audience and validating your business idea.

1.   Better Understanding of Target Audience: By conducting market research, you gain a deeper understanding of your target audience, their needs, wants, and behaviors. This information will help you tailor your product or service to their needs and create a solution that they will love.

2.   Validate Your Business Idea: Market research helps you validate your business idea by testing it to see if there is a demand for your product or service. This will

help you avoid costly mistakes and ensure that your business is solving a real problem.

3. Identify Market Opportunities: By researching your competitors and understanding the market, you can identify opportunities that you can exploit. This can lead to a competitive advantage and help you differentiate yourself from your competitors.

4. Improved Customer Satisfaction: By understanding your target audience and creating a product or service that meets their needs, you can improve customer satisfaction. This can lead to increased customer loyalty and positive word-of-mouth referrals.

5. Better Decision-Making: Market research provides valuable information that can inform your decision-making. By understanding your target audience and

market, you can make informed decisions about your business strategy, product development, and marketing efforts.

6.   Reduced Risk: Market research helps reduce the risk of starting a business by providing information about the viability of your idea and the demand for your product or service. This information can help you make more informed decisions and avoid costly mistakes.

Market research provides numerous advantages in understanding your target audience and validating your business idea. It's important to invest time and effort into market research to ensure the success of your business.

Not conducting market research can result in several disadvantages for your business, such as:

1.   Missed Opportunities: Without market research, you may miss out on identifying opportunities in the market. This can result in missed sales and missed chances to differentiate yourself from your competitors.

2.   Poor Product-Market Fit: Without understanding your target audience and market, you may develop a product or service that doesn't meet their needs. This can result in poor sales and customer dissatisfaction.

3.   Wasted Resources: Starting a business without conducting market research can result in wasted resources, such as time, money, and effort. This is because you may be developing a product or service that

doesn't have a market, or you may be missing out on opportunities to improve your business.

4. Inaccurate Financial Projections: Without market research, your financial projections may be inaccurate. This can result in underfunding or overfunding, which can negatively impact your business.

5. Increased Risk: Not conducting market research increases the risk of starting a business. Without understanding your target audience and market, you may make costly mistakes that can harm your business.

6. Missed Customer Needs: Without understanding your target audience, you may miss out on their needs and wants. This can result in a product or service that doesn't meet their needs, leading to poor customer satisfaction and negative word-of-mouth referrals.

Not conducting market research can result in several disadvantages for your business. It's important to invest time and effort into market research to ensure the success of your business and avoid costly mistakes

In conclusion, market research is a crucial step in starting a business. By conducting market research, you can gain a better understanding of your target audience, validate your business idea, identify market opportunities, improve customer satisfaction, and make informed decisions. On the other hand, not conducting market research can result in missed opportunities, poor product-market fit, wasted resources, inaccurate financial projections, increased risk, and missed customer needs. To ensure the success of your business, it's important to invest time and effort into market research and understand your target audience. This will give you a competitive advantage and help you create a product or service that meets their needs and solves their problems.

CHAPTER THREE

"The Blueprint: Crafting Your Business Plan"

A business plan is a comprehensive document that outlines the goals, strategies, and financial projections of a business. It is a critical tool for entrepreneurs who are starting a new business or seeking investment, as it provides a roadmap for success and helps secure funding from investors and lenders. A business plan is also an important resource for established businesses, as it can be used to measure progress and make informed decisions about growth and expansion.

The main purpose of a business plan is to provide a clear and concise overview of your business, including its objectives, target market, marketing strategies, financial projections, and organizational structure. It should also outline any potential risks and challenges your business may face and how you plan to mitigate them. The business plan should provide a complete picture of your business and its potential for success, and it should be written in a way that is clear, concise, and easy to understand.

A well-written business plan should be comprehensive, covering all aspects of your business from its product or service offerings, to its marketing strategies, to its financial projections. This level of detail is necessary to convince investors and lenders that your business is a sound investment. A business plan should be dynamic and flexible, and it should be updated regularly to reflect changes in the business environment and the company's progress. A well-designed business plan is not only a tool for securing funding, but it is also a valuable management tool that can help you stay on track and reach your goals over time.

In addition to securing funding, a well-written business plan can also help you attract and retain talented employees. A comprehensive plan that outlines the company's goals, strategies, and financial projections can help employees see the future of the company and understand how their work fits into the big picture. A business plan can also serve as a reference for employees and can help keep everyone on the same page, aligned with the company's goals and objectives.

Another important aspect of a business plan is the financial projections. In this section, you will outline your revenue, expenses, and cash flow projections for the next several years. Financial projections are important for attracting investors and lenders, as they demonstrate the potential profitability of your business. They also provide a roadmap for your company's financial future, which is essential for making informed business decisions.

In conclusion, a business plan is a critical tool for starting and running a successful business. It provides a roadmap for success, outlines the goals and strategies of your business, and demonstrates the potential profitability of your company. A well-written business plan is a valuable resource for entrepreneurs, investors, and lenders, and it can help you attract and retain talented employees. Whether you're starting a new business or expanding an existing one, a business plan is an essential tool for success

Here is a breakdown on how you can design your business plan:

Step 1: Executive Summary The executive summary is a brief overview of your business plan. It should be no longer than two pages and should include a description of your business, its goals, and the strategies you will use to achieve them. This section should be written last, after you have completed the rest of your business plan, as it provides a summary of the key points you have made.

Step 2: Company Description In this section, you will provide a detailed description of your business, including its history, the products or services you offer, your mission statement, and the problem your business solves. This section should also include information about your management team, including their experience and qualifications.

Step 3: Market Analysis In this section, you will conduct a thorough analysis of your target market. This includes information about the size of your target market, your competitors, and the strengths and weaknesses of your business in comparison to your competitors. This information will help you understand your target market and develop strategies to differentiate yourself from your competitors.

Step 4: Product or Service Line In this section, you will describe your product or service in detail, including its features and benefits. You will also provide information about your pricing strategy and any warranties or guarantees you offer. This section should also include information about your production process, including the materials and equipment you will use.

Step 5: Marketing and Sales In this section, you will describe your marketing and sales strategies, including how you will reach your target audience and how you will generate sales. This section should also include information about your pricing strategy, sales channels, and marketing budget.

Step 6: Financial Projections In this section, you will provide financial projections for your business, including your sales forecast, expenses, and profitability. This section should also include information about your start-up costs, including the cost of equipment, inventory, and marketing. You should also include a break-even analysis, which shows when your business will become profitable.

Step 7: Funding In this section, you will describe your funding requirements, including the amount of capital you need to start your business and the sources of funding you plan to use. This section should also include information about your use of funds, including how you will use the capital you raise.

Step 8: Conclusion In the conclusion of your business plan, you should summarize the key points you have made and provide a summary of your business and its goals. You should also include a call-to-action, encouraging your reader to take action and invest in your business.

Crafting a comprehensive business plan is an essential step in starting a successful business. A well-written business plan will provide a roadmap for your business and help you achieve your goals. It should include a detailed description of your business, market analysis, product or service line, marketing and sales strategies, financial projections, and funding requirements. By following these steps, you can create a blueprint for your business and increase your chances of success.

A good business plan is of multiple benefits, let's take a look at some of them.

A business plan is a key document that outlines the goals, strategies, and financial projections of a business. It is an essential tool for entrepreneurs who are starting a new business or seeking investment, as it provides a roadmap for success and helps secure funding from investors and lenders. A business plan is also an important resource for established businesses, as it can be used to measure progress and make informed decisions about growth and expansion.

One of the primary benefits of having a business plan is that it forces you to think critically about every aspect of your business. By carefully considering and documenting your goals, strategies, target market, marketing plan, organizational structure, and financial projections, you are able to identify potential problems and opportunities that you may not have otherwise considered. This level of detail and forethought can help you avoid common pitfalls and ensure the success of your business.

Another important benefit of having a business plan is that it can help you secure funding from investors and lenders. A comprehensive and well-written business plan is essential for convincing potential investors and lenders that your business is a sound investment. A business plan that demonstrates the potential profitability of your company and outlines a clear path for growth and success is much more likely to secure funding than a poorly thought out or poorly written plan.

In addition to securing funding, a business plan can also help you attract and retain talented employees. A comprehensive plan that outlines the company's goals, strategies, and financial projections can help employees see the future of the company and understand how their work fits into the big picture. A business plan can also serve as a reference for employees and can help keep everyone on the same page, aligned with the company's goals and objectives.

A business plan can also help you measure progress and make informed decisions about growth and expansion. By comparing actual results to your financial projections and business goals, you can determine what is working well and what needs to be changed. This information can be used to make informed decisions about expanding your business, launching new products or services, or making changes to your marketing strategies.

There could be serious consequences if you do not have a business plan

A business plan is a crucial document for any business, big or small. Without a well-crafted business plan, a business is likely to face several consequences that could negatively impact its success. Here are some of the most significant consequences of not drafting a business plan:

1.   Lack of direction: A business plan provides a clear direction for the business, helping entrepreneurs to determine their goals, strategies, and objectives. Without a business plan, a business may lack a clear sense of direction, making it more challenging to achieve its goals.

2. Poor allocation of resources: A business plan helps entrepreneurs to make informed decisions about how to allocate their resources effectively. Without a business plan, a business may waste its resources on unproductive activities, which could have a negative impact on its bottom line.

3. Difficulty in securing funding: Many investors and lenders require a business plan before they will consider providing funding. Without a business plan, it will be challenging for a business to secure the funding it needs to grow and succeed.

4. Increased risk of failure: A business plan helps entrepreneurs to anticipate and mitigate risks that could threaten the success of the business. Without a

business plan, a business is likely to be more vulnerable to these risks, which could lead to failure.

5.   Inability to measure success: A business plan includes metrics that can be used to measure the success of the business. Without a business plan, it will be challenging to determine if the business is on track to achieve its goals, which could limit its ability to make informed decisions about how to improve.

In conclusion, not having a business plan can have severe consequences for a business, including a lack of direction, poor allocation of resources, difficulty in securing funding, increased risk of failure, and an inability to measure success. It is critical for entrepreneurs to take the time to draft a comprehensive business plan to ensure the success of their business.

I hope now you realize that a business plan is an essential tool for starting and running a successful business. It provides a roadmap for success, outlines the goals and strategies of your business, and demonstrates the potential profitability of your company. A well-written business plan is a valuable resource for entrepreneurs, investors, and lenders, and it can help you attract and retain talented employees. Whether you're starting a new business or expanding an existing one, a business plan is a critical component of success.

CHAPTER FOUR

"Brand Building: Creating a Unique Identity"

Brand building is a critical aspect of building a successful business. Your brand is the sum total of all your customers' experiences with your company, and it is the key to creating a unique identity that sets you apart from your competitors. In this chapter, we will explore the importance of brand building and the steps you can take to create a strong, recognizable brand for your business.

The first step in brand building is to define your brand's mission, vision, and values. Your mission statement should reflect the purpose of your business and the benefits you offer to your customers. Your vision statement should outline what you hope to achieve in the future, and your values should reflect the principles that guide your business decisions.

Once you have defined your brand's mission, vision, and values, it's time to create a brand strategy. Your brand strategy should include a detailed description of your target audience, your unique value proposition, and your brand positioning. This information will help you make informed decisions about your branding, marketing, and communication efforts, and will ensure that your brand messaging is consistent across all channels.

One of the most important aspects of brand building is creating a consistent visual identity. This includes designing a logo and visual elements that are representative of your brand and consistent across all marketing materials. Your visual identity should be memorable, distinctive, and reflective of your brand's mission, vision, and values.

Another key component of brand building is building brand awareness and recognition. This involves reaching your target audience through marketing and advertising efforts and consistently delivering on your brand promise. Establishing a strong online presence through a well-designed website and active social media accounts is also critical for building brand awareness and connecting with your target audience.

Finally, it's important to regularly evaluate and adjust your brand building efforts. This involves monitoring your brand's performance, tracking key metrics such as brand awareness and customer loyalty, and making changes as needed to ensure that your brand remains relevant and appealing to your target audience.

In conclusion, brand building is a critical component of building a successful business. It is the key to creating a unique identity and differentiating your business from your competitors. By defining your brand's mission, vision, and values, creating a consistent visual identity, building brand awareness, and regularly evaluating and adjusting your efforts, you can create a strong, recognizable brand that resonates with your target audience.

Brand building is of great importance. Let's take a look at some of the importance.

1.   Competitive Advantage: One of the most critical advantages of having a unique brand identity is that it helps a business stand out in a crowded marketplace. A well-established brand identity can differentiate a business from its competitors and make it easier for customers to remember and recognize the company. This increased recognition can lead to increased brand loyalty, higher sales, and a competitive edge in the market.

2.   Customer Loyalty: A strong brand identity can help to create an emotional connection with customers, which can lead to increased customer loyalty. When customers feel a connection with a brand, they are more likely to become repeat customers and recommend the brand to others. This type of customer loyalty is

invaluable to a business and can help to increase revenue and profits over time.

3.   Credibility and Trust: A well-crafted brand identity can help a business establish credibility and trust with customers. A credible and trustworthy brand can increase customer confidence in the business, which can lead to increased sales and improved customer relationships.

4.   Consistency: A strong brand identity helps to create consistency in the way a business presents itself to customers. Consistency in messaging, visual elements, and tone of voice can help to create a recognizable and memorable brand that customers can rely on.

5.   Long-term Success: Building a unique brand identity is an investment in the long-term success of a

business. A well-established brand identity can provide a business with a competitive advantage, increased customer loyalty, improved credibility, and a foundation for future growth. By taking the time to create a unique brand identity, a business can position itself for success and achieve its long-term goals.

Take a good look at this story:

There was a small business called "Sophie's Sweets." Sophie was a talented baker who made the most delicious cakes, cookies, and pastries in town. She started her business from her home kitchen and soon became known for her delicious treats. People in the neighborhood would stop by to buy her sweets, and word quickly spread about the quality of Sophie's products.

However, as the business grew, Sophie realized that she needed to do something to make her business stand out from all the other bakeries in town. She knew that if she didn't take action, her business would *get lost in the crowd* and eventually fail.

So, Sophie decided to invest in building her brand. She hired a branding expert who helped her define her brand values and mission. Together, they created a visual identity for the business and a brand strategy that reflected Sophie's passion for baking and her commitment to using only the finest ingredients.

With the help of her branding expert, Sophie also focused on building brand awareness by launching a social media campaign, participating in local food fairs, and working with food bloggers to promote her products.

The results were remarkable. Sophie's customers became more loyal, and new customers started to discover her business. People were talking about Sophie's Sweets, and the business was growing at a faster pace than ever before.

Sophie was thrilled with the results and realized that investing in her brand was one of the best decisions she had ever made. She learned that building a strong brand not only helped her business stand out from the competition, but it also helped her connect with her customers on a deeper level and build a loyal following.

In the end, Sophie's Sweets became one of the most successful bakeries in the city, and Sophie was proud to be known as the baker who created a brand that was both delicious and unique.

Creating a unique brand identity is an essential aspect of marketing and business success. A strong brand identity can provide a business with a competitive advantage, increased customer loyalty, improved credibility, consistency, and a foundation for long-term success. By taking the time to build a strong brand, a business can position itself for success and achieve its goals in the market.

Not building a brand is a mistake that many businesses make, and it can have several significant disadvantages. Here are some of the most significant disadvantages of not building a brand:

1. Lack of recognition: Without a brand, a business may struggle to be recognized in a crowded marketplace. This lack of recognition can lead to decreased brand loyalty and lower sales.

2. Increased competition: A lack of brand differentiation can make it more challenging for a business to stand out from its competitors. This increased competition can make it more difficult for a business to attract and retain customers.

3. Decreased customer loyalty: Without a brand, a business may struggle to create an emotional connection with customers. This lack of emotional connection can lead to decreased customer loyalty and a higher risk of customers switching to competitors.

4.   Decreased credibility: Without a well-crafted brand, a business may struggle to establish credibility and trust with customers. This decreased credibility can lead to decreased customer confidence and lower sales.

5.   Lack of consistency: Without a brand, a business may struggle to maintain consistency in the way it presents itself to customers. This lack of consistency can lead to confusion and a decreased ability to establish a recognizable and memorable brand.

In conclusion, not building a brand can have several significant disadvantages, including a lack of recognition, increased competition, decreased customer loyalty, decreased credibility, and a lack of consistency.

It is crucial for businesses to invest in building a strong brand to ensure their success in the market.

How to build a brand

1.   Define your brand values and mission: To build a strong brand, it is essential to have a clear understanding of your brand values and mission. This includes identifying what sets your brand apart from others, what your brand stands for, and what it hopes to achieve. Your brand values and mission should be reflected in all of your marketing materials and communication efforts.

2.   Develop a brand strategy: Once you have a clear understanding of your brand values and mission, the next step is to develop a brand strategy. This includes defining your target audience, determining your unique

selling proposition, and creating a brand messaging platform. A well-defined brand strategy will help to guide your brand-building efforts and ensure that your brand is consistent and cohesive.

3.   Create a visual identity: A strong visual identity is essential to building a successful brand. This includes designing a logo, creating a color palette, and establishing typography standards. Your visual identity should be consistent across all of your marketing materials and should accurately reflect your brand values and mission.

4.   Build brand awareness: Building brand awareness is critical to the success of your brand. This can be achieved through various marketing efforts, such as digital advertising, social media marketing, content

marketing, and public relations. The goal of brand awareness efforts is to reach your target audience and introduce them to your brand.

5.   Consistency is key: Maintaining consistency in all aspects of your brand is crucial to building a strong brand identity. This includes consistency in visual elements, messaging, and tone of voice. Consistency will help to create a recognizable and memorable brand that customers can rely on.

In conclusion, building a brand requires a clear understanding of your brand values and mission, a well-defined brand strategy, a strong visual identity, a focus on building brand awareness, and a commitment to consistency. By following these steps, businesses can build a strong brand that will differentiate them from their competitors and help them to achieve success in the market.

CHAPTER FIVE

"Raising Capital: Securing Funding for Your Startup"

Raising capital is one of the biggest challenges that startups face. It can be difficult to secure funding when you're just starting out and have no track record or established brand. However, with careful planning and strategy, it is possible to secure the funding you need to launch and grow your business. In this chapter, we'll take a detailed look at the various options available to startups looking to raise capital.

1. Bootstrapping: Bootstrapping refers to starting a business with little to no outside funding. This is often achieved by using personal savings, credit cards, or loans from family and friends. While bootstrapping

can be a good option for businesses with low overhead costs, it is not a viable option for businesses that require significant upfront investment.

2.   Angel Investors: Angel investors are high net worth individuals who invest in startups in exchange for ownership equity. Angel investors can provide startups with significant capital, mentorship, and industry contacts. To attract angel investors, startups need to have a solid business plan, a unique product or service, and a compelling pitch.

3.   Venture Capital: Venture capital is a type of equity financing that is provided by venture capital firms. These firms invest in startups with high growth potential in exchange for ownership equity. Venture capital is

typically provided to businesses that have a proven track record of success and are at a later stage of development.

4.   Crowdfunding: Crowdfunding is a method of raising capital by soliciting small investments from a large number of people. Crowdfunding campaigns can be conducted online through platforms such as Kickstarter or Indiegogo. Crowdfunding is a good option for startups that have a compelling story and a large social media following.

5.   Bank Loans: Bank loans are a traditional source of funding for businesses. Banks provide loans based on the creditworthiness of the borrower and the potential for repayment. Bank loans can be secured or unsecured, and interest rates vary based on the terms of the loan.

6.   Grants: Grants are a type of funding that is provided by government agencies, foundations, or corporations. Grants are typically provided to businesses that are focused on addressing specific social or environmental problems. To receive a grant, businesses must submit a proposal and demonstrate their eligibility.

7.   IPO (Initial Public Offering): An IPO is a way for startups to raise capital by selling shares of stock to the public. An IPO allows startups to raise large amounts of capital and provides liquidity to existing investors. However, going public is a complex and expensive process, and is typically only considered by startups that have achieved significant growth and profitability.

In conclusion, there are many options available to startups looking to raise capital. The best option will depend on the specific needs and goals of your business. When deciding on a funding strategy, it is important to consider the amount of control you are willing to give up, the level of risk you are comfortable with, and the resources you have available. By carefully considering these factors, you can make informed decisions about how to raise the capital you need to launch and grow your business.

It is important to note that securing funding is not just about finding the right source of capital, but also about having a solid plan in place to use that capital effectively. Here are some tips for developing a strong plan for using the funds you raise:

1.	Define Your Goals: Before you start raising capital, it is important to have a clear understanding of what you want to achieve with the funds. This could be anything from hiring a team, developing a new product, or expanding into new markets. Make sure that your goals are realistic, achievable, and aligned with your overall business strategy.

2.	Develop a Budget: Once you have defined your goals, you need to develop a budget that outlines how you plan to allocate the funds you raise. This budget should include all of your expected expenses, including salaries, marketing costs, and equipment purchases. Make sure that your budget is realistic and that you have a contingency plan in place for unexpected expenses.

3.   Create a Financial Projection: A financial projection is a forecast of your future financial performance based on your current business model and assumptions about the future. This projection should include a detailed breakdown of your expected revenue and expenses, as well as a projection of your cash flow. This will help you understand whether your business is likely to generate enough revenue to repay the funds you raise.

4.   Show Evidence of Traction: Investors are more likely to invest in a business that has already shown some traction. This could be in the form of revenue, customer growth, or user engagement. Make sure that you have evidence of traction to show potential investors,

and that you can clearly communicate the potential for future growth.

5.   Build a Strong Team: Investors are not just investing in your business, they are also investing in your team. Make sure that you have a strong and experienced team in place, and that you are able to demonstrate the skills and expertise of your team members. Consider hiring key employees or advisors to help build your team and demonstrate your commitment to success.

6.   Build a Strong Network: Building a strong network of advisors, mentors, and investors is key to securing funding and growing your business. Make sure that you are regularly connecting with potential investors and advisors, and that you are actively seeking out opportunities to network and build relationships.

It's also important to understand the different sources of funding available for startups and to choose the right one for your business. Here are some of the most common sources of funding:

It's also important to consider the terms and conditions of the funding you are receiving, as well as the equity you are giving up. Make sure you have a clear understanding of the terms of the funding and that you are comfortable with the equity you are giving up. It's also important to understand the implications of taking on debt or selling equity, and to have a solid plan in place for using the funds you raise.

In addition to securing funding, it's important to have a strong plan in place for using the funds effectively. This includes developing a budget, creating a financial projection, and having a clear understanding of your goals and how you plan to achieve them. With the right planning and execution, you can secure the funding you need to launch and grow your business.

Another important aspect of raising capital is to have a well-crafted pitch and presentation that clearly communicates your vision and the value proposition of your business. The pitch should include the following elements:

1.   Introduction: Start by introducing yourself, your co-founders, and your team, and briefly describe the background and expertise of each person.

2.   Problem: Clearly state the problem your business is solving and why it's a significant issue.

3.   Solution: Explain your solution to the problem, including the key features and benefits of your product or service.

4.   Market Opportunity: Describe the market opportunity for your business, including the size of the market and your target customer segments.

5.   Business Model: Explain your business model, including how you plan to generate revenue, your pricing strategy, and your marketing and sales channels.

6.   Financial Projections: Provide a clear and detailed financial projection, including your revenue

projections, operating expenses, and capital requirements.

7. Team: Highlight the strengths of your team, including your background and expertise, and explain how you plan to use your team to execute your vision.

8. Ask: Clearly state what you are asking for and why it's important to your business.

Your pitch should be concise, compelling, and well-prepared, and should clearly communicate the value of your business and why it's a good investment opportunity.

In addition to having a well-crafted pitch, it's vital to have a clear understanding of the legal and regulatory aspects of raising capital. This includes understanding the laws and regulations surrounding equity crowdfunding, private placement offerings, and public offerings, and making sure you comply with all relevant regulations.

Raising capital is a critical component of starting and growing a successful business. It provides the resources needed to fund the development of products and services, hire staff, and invest in marketing and sales efforts. The importance of raising capital cannot be overstated, as it plays a crucial role in the growth and success of any business.

One of the main benefits of raising capital is that it enables businesses to scale quickly. With access to more resources, businesses can invest in the development of new products and services, expand into new markets, and hire additional staff to support growth. This can help businesses to stay ahead of the competition and build a strong market position.

Another important benefit of raising capital is that it can help businesses to manage their cash flow more effectively. With a steady stream of capital, businesses can ensure that they have the resources they need to cover operating costs, invest in growth initiatives, and weather any economic downturns. This helps businesses to stay financially stable and avoid the risk of bankruptcy or insolvency.

Raising capital also helps businesses to attract and retain top talent. With access to additional resources, businesses can offer competitive salaries and benefits packages, and create a positive work environment that attracts and retains top-performing employees. This can help businesses to build a strong and dedicated team, which is essential for long-term success.

Finally, raising capital can also help businesses to build credibility and legitimacy in the eyes of investors, customers, and partners. When a business has access to capital, it sends a signal to the market that it is a legitimate and viable operation, and that it has the resources to achieve its goals. This can help businesses to attract new investment, customers, and partnerships, which can be critical for growth and success.

In conclusion, raising capital is a critical component of starting and growing a successful business. With access to additional resources, businesses can scale quickly, manage their cash flow more effectively, attract and retain top talent, and build credibility and legitimacy in the eyes of investors, customers, and partners. By prioritizing the process of raising capital, businesses can ensure that they have the resources they need to achieve their goals and succeed in the long term.

CHAPTER SIX

"Building Your Team: Hiring the Right People"

Building a strong and dedicated team is one of the most important aspects of starting and growing a successful business. The right team can make all the difference in achieving success, while the wrong team can be a major roadblock. Hiring the right people requires careful planning, strategic thinking, and a deep understanding of your business needs.

The first step in building your team is to define your hiring criteria and identify the skills, experiences, and personal qualities that are essential for success in your organization. This will help you to determine what type of candidates you should be targeting, and how you can assess their fit for your company.

Once you have a clear understanding of your hiring criteria, you can start the process of recruiting and hiring. There are many different recruitment channels to consider, including online job boards, social media, and employee referrals. Consider what works best for your business, and make sure to use a combination of channels to maximize your reach.

When you receive a candidate's application, take the time to carefully review their resume and cover letter. If their experience and qualifications seem to match your needs, schedule an interview to learn more about their skills, experiences, and personal qualities.

During the interview, ask questions that will help you to understand their work style, personality, and fit for your company culture. You can also ask them to provide examples of how they have handled challenging situations in the past, and how they have contributed to the success of their previous teams.

If you are impressed by a candidate's skills, experience, and personal qualities, consider making them a job offer. When making an offer, be clear about the salary and benefits package, as well as any expectations for performance and advancement within the company.

Once you have hired a new employee, it's important to provide them with the support and resources they need to succeed. This may include providing them with training and development opportunities, setting clear goals and expectations, and providing regular feedback and coaching.

Another important aspect of building your team is to create a positive and supportive work environment. This means fostering a culture of open communication, collaboration, and inclusiveness. A positive work environment can help to increase employee engagement, reduce turnover, and improve overall productivity.

One effective way to create a positive work environment is to involve your employees in the decision-making process. This can help to build trust and increase their investment in the success of the company. You can also involve your employees in the development of company policies, processes, and strategies, and seek their input and feedback on important issues.

It's also important to recognize and reward your employees for their hard work and achievements. This can be done through formal recognition programs, such as employee of the month awards, or informal gestures, such as a shout-out during a team meeting or a thank you note.

Another aspect of building a strong team is to provide opportunities for professional growth and development. This can help to retain your best employees and increase their engagement and productivity. You can offer training and development programs, mentorship opportunities, and leadership positions within the company.

Building a strong team is crucial for the success of a business. A team is the backbone of any organization, and a weak team can lead to the downfall of even the most promising venture. On the other hand, a strong and cohesive team can help a business overcome obstacles, drive growth and achieve its goals. Here are some reasons why building a strong team is so important for a business.

First and foremost, a strong team helps to distribute the workload and increase productivity. When team members work together effectively, they can achieve more in less time. This allows the business to complete projects faster and with better results, which can result in increased revenue and growth. Moreover, a strong team can help to create a positive work environment, where team members feel motivated and inspired to do their best work.

Another key benefit of having a strong team is that it helps to foster innovation and creativity. When team members work together and share ideas, they can come up with new and creative solutions to problems that they may not have been able to solve on their own. This can lead to significant advancements and improvements in the business, which can give it a competitive advantage in the market.

In addition to fostering creativity, a strong team can also provide support and encouragement to its members. When team members feel supported and encouraged, they are more likely to take risks and try new things, which can lead to breakthroughs and success for the business. Additionally, a strong team can help to minimize conflicts and ensure that everyone is working towards a common goal.

Having a strong team can also help to build a sense of trust and loyalty among team members. When team members trust each other and are loyal to the business, they are more likely to stay with the company for the long-term. This can lead to stability and consistency in the workforce, which is important for the success and growth of the business.

Finally, it's important to be a good employer and treat your employees with respect and dignity. This includes following fair and ethical employment practices, providing a safe and healthy work environment, and complying with all applicable laws and regulations.

Building a strong business team is essential for the success and growth of an organization. A well-functioning team can increase productivity, foster innovation, provide support, and build trust and loyalty among team members. Here are some steps that can be taken to build a strong business team.

1.　　Define the team's goals and objectives: Before building a team, it's important to define the goals and objectives that the team will be working towards. This will help to ensure that everyone is aligned and working towards a common goal, which is key to building a strong team.

2.　　Hire the right people: The first step in building a strong team is to hire the right people. This means finding individuals who have the necessary skills, experience, and personality traits that align with the goals and values of the organization. It's important to take the time to thoroughly evaluate candidates before making a hire, as this can have a significant impact on the success of the team.

3. Foster open communication: Open and effective communication is key to building a strong team. Encourage team members to share their ideas and perspectives, and provide a safe and supportive environment where everyone feels comfortable sharing their thoughts. Regular team meetings and one-on-one check-ins can help to foster open communication and build trust among team members.

4. Provide training and development opportunities: Providing training and development

opportunities for team members can help to build their skills and increase their effectiveness. This can also help to foster a sense of growth and progress, which can be motivating for team members.

5.   Encourage teamwork and collaboration: Encouraging teamwork and collaboration can help to build a sense of unity and cohesiveness among team members. This can be done by setting up team-building activities, creating opportunities for cross-functional collaboration, and encouraging team members to work together on projects.

6.   Recognize and reward success: Recognizing and rewarding success is a key way to build a strong team. This can include things like offering bonuses, promotions, or other forms of recognition for exceptional

performance. When team members feel valued and appreciated, they are more likely to be motivated and engaged in their work.

7. Address conflicts promptly: Conflicts are inevitable in any team, but it's important to address them promptly to prevent them from escalating. Encourage team members to have open and honest discussions to resolve conflicts, and provide mediation if necessary.

Building a strong business team requires a combination of the right people, open communication, training and development opportunities, teamwork and collaboration, recognition and rewards, and prompt conflict resolution. By following these steps, businesses can build a strong and cohesive team that is well-positioned to drive success and growth.

In conclusion, building a strong team is essential for the success of a business. A strong team can increase productivity, foster innovation and creativity, provide support and encouragement, and build trust and loyalty among team members. Business owners and managers should prioritize building a strong team and invest time and resources into creating a positive and supportive work environment.

CHAPTER SEVEN

"Marketing Mastery: Getting Your Product in Front of Customers"

Marketing mastery is a crucial aspect of any successful business as it helps to bring your product in front of customers and reach your target market. Whether you are a small startup or a large corporation, it is essential to have a strong marketing strategy in place to reach your desired audience and achieve your business goals.

Market mastery refers to the ability to effectively understand and reach your target market through marketing strategies. It involves understanding the needs, wants, and preferences of your target market and creating a marketing plan to reach and engage them. Market mastery is about understanding your customers and creating a customer-centric marketing plan that meets their needs and drives growth for your business.

Market mastery requires a deep understanding of your target market, including their demographics, purchasing habits, and motivations. This knowledge can be used to create a marketing strategy that effectively reaches your target market and promotes your product. Market mastery also requires a deep understanding of marketing channels and tactics, including digital marketing, content marketing, social media marketing, and traditional advertising. By using these channels effectively, you can reach your target market and promote your product to drive growth for your business.

Market mastery also requires a deep understanding of your brand and the unique value proposition it offers. This understanding can be used to create a compelling brand message and establish a strong brand identity that resonates with your target market. Market mastery requires a focus on the customer experience, from the first point of contact with your business to post-purchase follow-up. By providing a seamless and enjoyable customer experience, you can build customer loyalty and drive repeat business, which is essential for long-term success.

Market mastery is about understanding your target market and creating a marketing strategy that effectively reaches and engages them. It requires a deep understanding of your target market, marketing channels and tactics, and your brand. Market mastery is a critical aspect of any successful business as it drives awareness, generates leads and sales, enhances the customer experience, and enhances your reputation as a business.

Here are seven extensive importance of marketing mastery:

1. Drive Awareness and Interest: Marketing mastery is crucial for driving awareness and interest in your product. By effectively promoting your product, you can reach a wider audience and generate interest among potential customers. Marketing mastery can help you to effectively communicate the value of your product and establish a clear and compelling brand message.

2.   Build Credibility and Trust: Effective marketing is essential for building credibility and trust with your target market. A strong marketing strategy can help you to establish your brand as a leader in your industry and demonstrate your expertise and commitment to delivering high-quality products. This can help to build trust with potential customers and establish a strong reputation for your business.

3.   Increase Sales and Revenue: Marketing mastery is critical for increasing sales and revenue for your business. By effectively reaching your target market and promoting your product, you can increase the number of customers who purchase your product and drive growth for your business. Effective marketing can also help you to increase the average order value and

customer lifetime value, which can drive long-term success for your business.

4.   Enhance Customer Experience: Marketing mastery can help to enhance the customer experience by providing customers with the information they need to make informed decisions about your product. By effectively communicating the features and benefits of your product, you can help customers to understand the value of your product and make informed purchasing decisions. A strong marketing strategy can also help to create a seamless customer journey, from the first point of contact with your business to post-purchase follow-up, which can drive customer loyalty and repeat business.

5.   Compete with Competitors: Marketing mastery is essential for competing with your competitors

in your industry. By effectively promoting your product and differentiating your brand, you can establish a competitive advantage and reach your target market before your competitors. Effective marketing can also help you to stay ahead of industry trends and meet the changing needs of your target market.

6. Generate Leads and Sales: Marketing mastery is critical for generating leads and sales for your business. By effectively reaching your target market and promoting your product, you can generate leads and interest among potential customers. Effective marketing can also help you to nurture leads and convert them into paying customers, driving growth for your business.

7. Enhance Your Reputation: Marketing mastery is essential for enhancing your reputation as a

business. By effectively promoting your product and establishing a strong brand identity, you can build credibility and trust with your target market. A strong marketing strategy can also help you to establish a reputation for delivering high-quality products and exceptional customer service, which can drive long-term success for your business.

Here are some key elements of marketing mastery that you should consider:

1.   Know Your Target Market: Understanding your target market is crucial for effective marketing. You should take the time to research and understand your customers' needs, interests, and behaviors. This information can be used to create targeted marketing

campaigns that are tailored to your audience and more likely to resonate with them.

2.   Develop a Unique Value Proposition: A unique value proposition is a clear and concise statement that sets your product apart from your competition. It highlights the key benefits and features of your product and why it is the best choice for your target market. A strong value proposition can help you to capture the attention of your target market and stand out from your competition.

3.   Leverage Multiple Marketing Channels: Relying on a single marketing channel is not enough to reach your target market effectively. Instead, you should use a combination of marketing channels, including traditional advertising, content marketing, social media

marketing, email marketing, and search engine optimization (SEO), to reach your target market. Each channel has its own strengths and weaknesses, so it's important to determine which channels are most effective for your business and focus your marketing efforts accordingly.

4.   Create Engaging Content: Content is the backbone of any successful marketing campaign. You should aim to create content that is relevant, valuable, and engaging for your target market. This can include blog posts, videos, infographics, case studies, and other types of content that can help to build awareness and interest in your product.

5.   Measure and Optimize Your Marketing Efforts: Measuring the success of your marketing efforts

is critical for continuous improvement. You should use analytics tools and metrics to track the performance of your marketing campaigns, such as website traffic, conversion rates, and return on investment (ROI). This information can be used to optimize your marketing campaigns and make data-driven decisions to improve your marketing results.

6. Build Relationships with Your Target Market: Building strong relationships with your target market is key to long-term success. You should aim to engage with your customers regularly and provide value to them in various ways. This can include providing helpful resources, offering promotions, and responding to customer inquiries and feedback in a timely and professional manner.

7.   Continuously Test and Experiment: The world of marketing is constantly evolving, so it's important to stay up-to-date with the latest trends and techniques. You should continuously test and experiment with new marketing strategies and techniques to determine what works best for your business. This can help you to stay ahead of the curve and stay relevant in the ever-changing marketing landscape. By mastering the art of marketing, you can drive significant growth and success for your business. In addition to the key elements outlined above, here are a few additional tips to help you achieve marketing mastery:

8.   Develop a Strong Brand Identity: Your brand identity is the foundation of your marketing efforts. It is the image that represents your business and is

communicated to your target market through your logo, messaging, and marketing materials. A strong brand identity can help to build trust and credibility with your target market and set you apart from your competition.

9.   Utilize Influencer Marketing: Influencer marketing is a powerful tool that involves partnering with influencers in your industry to promote your product. Influencer marketing can help you reach a wider audience, build brand awareness, and increase credibility and trust with your target market. When choosing influencers to work with, it is important to choose those who align with your brand values and have a strong following among your target market.

10.   Stay Ahead of Industry Trends: Staying ahead of industry trends is critical for success in

marketing. By staying up-to-date with the latest trends, you can stay relevant and adapt your marketing strategies to meet the changing needs of your target market. You should regularly attend industry conferences, read industry publications, and network with other professionals in your industry to stay informed on the latest trends and developments.

11. Focus on Customer Experience: The customer experience is a critical component of your marketing efforts. You should aim to create a seamless and positive customer experience from start to finish, from the first point of contact with your business to post-purchase follow-up. This can include providing exceptional customer service, offering a user-friendly

website, and providing clear and concise product information.

12.   Foster a Customer-Centric Culture: Creating a customer-centric culture within your business is essential for marketing mastery. This means that every aspect of your business, from product development to customer service, should be focused on meeting the needs and expectations of your target market. By fostering a customer-centric culture, you can build strong relationships with your customers and drive long-term success for your business.

13.   Collaborate with Other Businesses: Collaborating with other businesses in your industry can be a powerful tool for marketing mastery. By partnering with complementary businesses, you can reach new

audiences, leverage each other's expertise and resources, and increase brand awareness and credibility. When choosing businesses to collaborate with, it is important to choose those that align with your values and share a similar target market.

14.   Invest in Marketing Automation: Marketing automation is a powerful tool that can help you streamline and optimize your marketing efforts. With marketing automation, you can automate repetitive tasks, such as email campaigns, lead nurturing, and social media updates, freeing up more time to focus on other important aspects of your business. Marketing automation can also help you to track and measure the performance of your marketing efforts and make data-driven decisions to improve your results.

In conclusion, marketing mastery is a critical aspect of any successful business. By effectively reaching your target market and promoting your product, you can drive awareness, build credibility and trust, increase sales and revenue, enhance the customer experience, compete with your competitors, generate leads and sales, and enhance your reputation as a business.

CHAPTER EIGHT

Operations Optimization: Streamlining Your Business   Processes

Operations optimization refers to the process of improving the efficiency and effectiveness of a business's operational processes. It involves identifying and eliminating inefficiencies and redundancies, streamlining processes, and implementing new technologies and systems to improve performance. The goal of operations optimization is to reduce costs, improve quality, and increase productivity, while also improving the overall customer experience.

Streamlining business processes is a key aspect of operations optimization. This involves analyzing the current processes in place and looking for ways to simplify or eliminate steps that are not necessary or add value to the customer. The objective is to make the process faster, more efficient, and easier to manage, while also reducing errors and improving customer satisfaction.

For example, a company may streamline its order fulfillment process by automating the tracking and management of orders from the time they are placed to the time they are delivered. By doing so, the company can reduce the time and effort required to manage orders, improve the accuracy of order tracking, and provide better customer service by providing real-time updates on order status. Operations optimization can be applied to all aspects of a business, including supply chain management, sales and marketing, and customer service, and can have a significant impact on a company's bottom line.

1.   Why is Operations Optimization Important?

Operations optimization is important for a number of reasons, including:

•   Increased Efficiency: Streamlining your business processes can increase efficiency and reduce waste, freeing up resources for other areas of your business.

•   Improved Productivity: By optimizing your business processes, you can improve productivity and reduce the time and resources required to complete tasks.

•   Enhanced Customer Experience: Optimizing your business processes can also enhance the customer experience by providing faster and more efficient service.

•   Cost Savings: Streamlining your business processes can result in cost savings by reducing waste and inefficiencies, freeing up resources for other areas of your business.

•   Competitive Advantage: Operations optimization can also give you a competitive advantage by allowing you to respond to changing market conditions and customer needs more quickly and effectively.

2.   Identifying Areas for Improvement

The first step in operations optimization is to identify areas for improvement. This involves reviewing your business processes and systems to identify inefficiencies and areas for improvement. Some common areas for improvement include:

•	Processes: Analyze your business processes to identify areas for improvement, such as eliminating unnecessary steps or streamlining procedures.

•	Systems: Evaluate your systems and technology to identify areas for improvement, such as upgrading software or implementing new technology to automate tasks.

•	Communication: Evaluate your communication processes to identify areas for improvement, such as improving cross-functional communication or implementing a more effective system for tracking and responding to customer inquiries.

3.   Implementing Changes

Once you have identified areas for improvement, the next step is to implement changes to streamline your business processes. This may involve:

•   Automating tasks: Automating tasks can increase efficiency and reduce the time and resources required to complete tasks.

•   Implementing new technology: Implementing new technology, such as project management software or customer relationship management (CRM) software, can help to streamline processes and improve productivity.

• Improving cross-functional communication: Improving cross-functional communication can help to ensure that everyone is on the same page and working towards a common goal.

4. Measuring Results

Measuring results is an important part of operations optimization. This involves tracking key metrics and performance indicators to determine the effectiveness of the changes you have made. Some key metrics to track include:

• Time savings: Track the time savings achieved by streamlining processes and implementing new technology.

• Cost savings: Track the cost savings achieved by reducing waste and inefficiencies.

• Customer satisfaction: Track customer satisfaction to determine the impact of the changes on the customer experience.

5. Continual Improvement

Operations optimization is a continuous process that requires ongoing attention and effort. This means that once you have implemented changes, you need to continue to monitor and improve your processes and systems to ensure that they remain efficient and effective.

6. Best Practices for Streamlining Your Business Processes

Some best practices for streamlining your business processes include:

• Focus on the customer experience: The customer experience should be at the forefront of all operations optimization efforts. This means that

• Involve employees: Involve employees in the optimization process by soliciting their feedback and ideas for improvement. This can help to increase buy-in and ensure that the changes you implement are practical and effective.

• Use data and analytics: Use data and analytics to make informed decisions about what changes to make and how to implement them. This can help to ensure that you are making the right decisions based on the facts, rather than just assumptions.

• Set clear goals: Set clear goals and objectives for the optimization process, and develop a plan to achieve them. This will help to ensure that you are focused on the right things and that you have a roadmap to follow.

• Continuously evaluate processes: Continuously evaluate your processes to identify areas for improvement and ensure that they are efficient and effective. This may involve regularly conducting process audits, benchmarking against industry standards, and conducting customer surveys to gather feedback.

• Encouraging employee creativity and innovation. Encourage employees to think outside of the box and come up with new ideas for improving processes. This can lead to breakthrough innovations that can significantly improve the efficiency and effectiveness of your business processes.

- Implementing a Lean or Six Sigma approach. Consider implementing a Lean or Six Sigma approach to operations optimization. These methodologies focus on eliminating waste, reducing variability, and improving quality. By following these methodologies, you can streamline processes, reduce costs, and improve overall business performance.

- Leveraging technology. Technology can play a critical role in operations optimization. From automating repetitive tasks to improving communication and collaboration, technology can help to streamline processes and increase efficiency. Consider implementing new technologies or upgrading existing systems to support your optimization efforts.

• Collaborating with suppliers and partners. Collaborating with suppliers and partners can also play a critical role in operations optimization. By working together to streamline processes and improve efficiency, you can achieve greater results and achieve your goals more quickly.

• Building cross-functional teams. Building cross-functional teams can also help to improve efficiency and streamline processes. Cross-functional teams bring together employees from different departments and areas of expertise to work on a common goal. This can lead to improved communication, greater collaboration, and better decision-making.

• Celebrating success. Finally, it is important to celebrate success and recognize the efforts of your employees. This can help to build morale and encourage employees to continue working towards continuous improvement.

In conclusion, operations optimization is an ongoing process that requires attention, effort, and dedication to achieve success. By streamlining processes, improving systems and technology, and fostering a culture of continuous improvement, you can increase efficiency, reduce costs, and improve overall business performance. With the right approach and commitment, you can master operations optimization and achieve your business goals.

CHAPTER NINE

"Scaling Success: Strategies for Growth"

Scaling a business from a small operation to a larger, more successful enterprise is a major challenge for any entrepreneur. Growth can bring new opportunities and increased revenue, but it also requires a new level of strategic planning and execution. In order to achieve sustainable growth, companies must understand the key drivers of their business, identify the barriers to growth, and implement effective strategies to overcome them.

1. Understanding Your Business Model: Before embarking on a growth strategy, it's crucial to have a clear understanding of your business model and how it generates revenue. This includes an analysis of your target market, your unique value proposition, and the

channels through which you reach customers. Understanding your business model will help you identify the key drivers of growth, such as increased sales, higher customer acquisition rates, and improved customer retention.

2: Identifying Barriers to Growth: Once you understand your business model, it's important to identify the barriers to growth that may be preventing you from reaching your full potential. These can include limited access to capital, lack of resources, competition, and limited market demand. Understanding the barriers to growth will help you prioritize your efforts and develop effective strategies to overcome them.

3: Developing a Growth Strategy: With a clear understanding of your business model and the barriers to growth, you can begin to develop a comprehensive growth strategy. This should include a clear definition of your target market and target customer segments, as well as a detailed plan for reaching those customers. Your growth strategy should also include a plan for expanding your product offerings, entering new markets, and leveraging technology to scale your business.

4: Building the Right Team: As your business grows, it's important to build the right team to support that growth. This includes hiring the right people, developing the necessary skills and capabilities, and creating a supportive culture that encourages collaboration and innovation. Building the right team will help ensure that you have the resources you need to execute your growth strategy effectively.

5: Securing the Right Partnerships and Alliances: Partnerships and alliances can play a critical role in helping your business scale and achieve sustainable growth. These relationships can provide access to new markets, resources, and expertise, as well as help you overcome barriers to growth. It's important to carefully evaluate potential partners and alliances, and choose those that align with your growth strategy and business goals.

6: Scaling Your Operations: As your business grows, it's important to scale your operations to keep pace. This includes investing in technology, automating processes, and streamlining operations to improve efficiency and reduce costs. Scaling your operations will help ensure that your business can handle the increased demand and continue to grow in a sustainable way.

The importance of Scaling Success: Strategies for Growth

1. Increases Revenue: One of the most important benefits of scaling success is the increase in revenue. A well-executed growth strategy can help businesses reach new markets and customers, which can result in increased sales and profits. With a focus on growth, businesses can leverage new opportunities and continue to generate revenue even in a challenging economic environment.

2.   Improves Competitive Advantage: Scaling success can also help businesses improve their competitive advantage by expanding their market reach and product offerings. A company that is growing and innovating will be better positioned to compete with larger, established businesses, and can differentiate itself in the marketplace by offering unique value to its customers.

3.   Attracts Investors: Investors are always looking for businesses that are growing and have a strong potential for future success. A well-executed growth strategy can help a business attract investment capital, which can be used to fund further growth and expansion. This can help businesses achieve their goals more quickly and effectively, and can also provide a significant return on investment for investors.

4.   Enhances Customer Experience: Scaling success can also have a positive impact on the customer experience. As a business grows, it can invest in new technologies and systems to improve the customer experience, such as enhanced online ordering systems or improved customer service capabilities. This can help businesses differentiate themselves from the competition and build loyalty among their customers.

5.   Facilitates Talent Retention: As businesses grow, they can offer their employees new opportunities for advancement and career development. This can help businesses retain their top talent and build a strong, motivated team. A focus on growth can also help businesses attract new talent, as employees are attracted to organizations that are growing and innovative.

6. Supports Sustainability: Finally, scaling success is critical for the long-term sustainability of a business. A focus on growth helps businesses stay ahead of market trends and changes, and allows them to continue to innovate and adapt to new challenges. This can help businesses maintain their competitive advantage and continue to generate revenue and profits well into the future.

Disadvantages of not Scaling Success: Strategies for Growth

1. Limited Market Reach: One of the biggest disadvantages of not scaling success is the limited market

reach that a business may experience. Without a focus on growth, a business may struggle to reach new customers and markets, which can limit its potential for success. In a highly competitive marketplace, a business that is not growing may find it difficult to compete with larger, more established businesses that have a wider reach.

2.   Decreased Revenue: Another major disadvantage of not scaling success is decreased revenue. Without a focus on growth, a business may struggle to generate the same level of sales and profits as it did in the past. This can result in decreased revenue, which can be a major challenge for any business, especially in a challenging economic environment.

3.   Missed Opportunities: Not scaling success can also result in missed opportunities. As the market changes and

evolves, businesses that are not growing may find themselves left behind and missing out on new opportunities for growth and success. This can limit the potential for future success and make it difficult for a business to achieve its goals.

4. Difficulty Attracting Talent: As businesses struggle to grow, they may also find it difficult to attract top talent. In today's competitive job market, employees are looking for opportunities to grow and develop their careers. If a business is not growing, it may not be seen as an attractive place to work, which can make it difficult to attract and retain top talent.

5. Decreased Customer Loyalty: A lack of growth can also have a negative impact on customer loyalty. If a business is not innovating and improving, its customers

may begin to look elsewhere for products and services that meet their needs. This can result in decreased customer loyalty and a decline in revenue.

6. Reduced Financial Health: Finally, a lack of growth can result in reduced financial health for a business. Without a focus on growth, a business may struggle to generate the revenue it needs to invest in new technologies, systems, and processes, which can limit its ability to remain competitive and successful in the long term.

Not scaling success can result in a number of significant disadvantages, including limited market reach, decreased revenue, missed opportunities, difficulty attracting talent, decreased customer loyalty, and reduced financial health. In order to achieve long-term success and remain competitive, it is critical for businesses to focus on growth and implement effective strategies for scaling success.

Scaling a business from a small operation to a larger, more successful enterprise is a major challenge, but it's also an exciting opportunity to achieve sustainable growth and achieve your goals. By understanding your business model, identifying barriers to growth, developing a comprehensive growth strategy, building the right team, securing the right partnerships and alliances, and scaling your operations, you can set your business on the path to success.

CHAPTER TEN

"Financial Management: Staying on Top of Your Finances"

Financial management is a crucial aspect of our personal and professional lives, and it is essential to stay on top of our finances to ensure financial stability and security. Good financial management enables us to create and maintain a healthy financial situation, save for the future, and achieve our financial goals.

Here are some tips for staying on top of your finances:

1.   Create a budget: The first step to staying on top of your finances is to create a budget. A budget is a plan that outlines your income and expenses, and helps you track your spending. It is important to review your

budget regularly to ensure you are staying within your means and making the most of your money.

2.   Track your spending: Keeping track of your spending is an essential part of financial management. It helps you see where your money is going and identify areas where you can cut back. There are many tools and apps available to help you track your spending, such as Personal Capital or Mint.

3.   Save regularly: Regular savings are critical to your financial stability and security. No matter how small the amount, setting aside a portion of your income for savings will help you build a safety net and achieve your financial goals. Consider setting up an automatic savings plan that moves a portion of your income into a savings account each month.

4.   Invest wisely: Investing is a key part of financial management, and it can help you grow your wealth over time. However, it is essential to invest wisely and understand the risks involved. Consider seeking the advice of a financial advisor or doing your own research before making investment decisions.

5.   Avoid debt: Debt can be a significant burden on your finances, and it is important to avoid it whenever possible. If you do need to take on debt, make sure you understand the terms and conditions and have a plan to pay it off. Credit card debt, in particular, can be expensive and accrue high-interest charges, so it is important to use credit cards responsibly.

6.   Plan for the future: Financial planning is crucial to ensure that you have a stable financial future. This

includes planning for your retirement, saving for a child's education, or buying a home. Consider seeking the advice of a financial advisor or using online resources to help you create a comprehensive financial plan.

Financial management is the process of managing your money to achieve financial stability and security. It involves creating a budget, tracking your expenses, saving regularly, investing wisely, avoiding debt, and planning for the future. By practicing good financial management, individuals can make the most of their money, achieve their financial goals, and prepare for the future.

A budget is a plan that outlines your income and expenses and helps you track your spending. It is important to review your budget regularly to make sure you are staying within your means and making the most of your money.

Tracking your expenses helps you see where your money is going and identify areas where you can cut back. There are many tools and apps available to help you track your spending, such as Personal Capital or Mint.

Saving regularly is critical to your financial stability and security. No matter how small the amount, setting aside a portion of your income for savings will help you build a safety net and achieve your financial goals.

Investing is a key part of financial management, and it can help you grow your wealth over time.

However, it is essential to invest wisely and understand the risks involved. Consider seeking the advice of a financial advisor or doing your own research before making investment decisions.

Debt can be a significant burden on your finances, and it is important to avoid it whenever possible. If you do need to take on debt, make sure you understand the terms and conditions and have a plan to pay it off.

Financial planning is crucial to ensure that you have a stable financial future. This includes planning for your retirement, saving for a child's education, or buying a home. Consider seeking the advice of a financial advisor or using online resources to help you create a comprehensive financial plan.

In conclusion, financial management is an essential aspect of our personal and professional lives that enables us to make the most of our money, achieve our financial goals, and prepare for the future. By practicing good financial management, individuals can enjoy financial stability and security.

The importance of financial management

Financial management is a critical aspect of our personal and professional lives that plays a crucial role in determining our financial stability and security. Good financial management skills enable individuals to make the most of their money, save for the future, and achieve their financial goals. Here are some of the importance of financial management.

1.   Helps in Better Money Management: Financial management is essential for better money management. It helps individuals understand their financial situation, track their expenses, and identify areas where they can cut back. With a good financial management system in place, individuals can prioritize their spending and make sure that their money is going where it is needed most.

2.   Aids in Achieving Financial Goals: Financial management is crucial for achieving financial goals, whether it is saving for retirement, buying a home, or paying off debt. Good financial management skills enable individuals to create a comprehensive financial plan, track their progress, and make adjustments as needed to achieve their financial goals.

3. Increases Savings and Wealth: Financial management plays a critical role in increasing savings and wealth. By tracking their spending, individuals can identify areas where they can cut back and redirect the saved money into a savings account. Regular savings and smart investments can help individuals build wealth over time and achieve financial stability and security.

4. Avoids Financial Stress and Burden: Good financial management can help individuals avoid financial stress and burden. It enables individuals to stay on top of their finances, avoid overspending, and avoid falling into debt. Financial management can also help individuals plan for the future and make sure that they are prepared for unexpected expenses, such as a medical emergency or a job loss.

5.   Enhances Credit Score: Financial management is also essential for maintaining a good credit score. A good credit score can make it easier for individuals to get approved for loans, credit cards, and mortgages. Good financial management skills, such as paying bills on time and avoiding debt, can help individuals maintain a good credit score and enjoy the benefits that come with it.

6.   Improves Financial Confidence and Security: Financial management can also help individuals feel more confident and secure about their finances. By understanding their financial situation and taking control of their finances, individuals can feel more secure and confident in their ability to manage their money and achieve their financial goals.

7.   Prepares for the Future: Financial management is crucial for preparing for the future. It helps individuals plan for unexpected events, such as a job loss or a medical emergency, and ensure that they have the resources they need to weather these events. Financial management can also help individuals prepare for retirement and ensure that they have the resources they need to enjoy their golden years.

Financial management is an essential aspect of our personal and professional lives that plays a crucial role in determining our financial stability and security. Good financial management skills enable individuals to make the most of their money, save for the future, achieve their financial goals, avoid financial stress and burden, and prepare for the future.

In conclusion, staying on top of your finances is essential to achieving financial stability and security. By creating a budget, tracking your spending, saving regularly, investing wisely, avoiding debt, and planning for the future, you can take control of your finances and achieve your financial goals. It is important to remember that financial management is a lifelong journey, and it is essential to be patient and disciplined to achieve financial success.

CHAPTER ELEVEN

"Overcoming Obstacles: Dealing with Challenges and Setbacks"

Overcoming obstacles and dealing with challenges and setbacks is a crucial aspect of personal and professional growth. These obstacles can range from lack of skills or resources, to external factors such as competition or personal problems. The key to overcoming these challenges is to identify the obstacle, develop a plan to overcome it, seek support, maintain a positive mindset, view failures as opportunities for growth and learning, and cultivate resilience.

Identifying the obstacle is the first step in overcoming it. Understanding the nature of the challenge is essential in developing a plan to overcome it. This may involve seeking advice or resources, developing new skills, or adjusting our approach.

Having a support system, such as friends, family, or a professional mentor or coach, can provide encouragement and motivation when facing challenges. Maintaining a positive attitude, surrounding ourselves with positive influences, and focusing on the things that bring us joy and fulfillment can help us stay motivated and optimistic.

It is important to view setbacks and failures as opportunities for growth and learning. Reflection on these challenges can help us develop new strategies and approaches that will help us overcome obstacles in the future. Celebrating progress and acknowledging milestones can help us stay motivated and focused on our goals.

Resilience is the ability to bounce back from setbacks and challenges. Cultivating resilience through positive thinking, seeking support when needed, and focusing on the things that bring us joy and fulfillment can help us overcome obstacles and achieve our goals.

1. Identify the Obstacle: The first step in overcoming an obstacle is to identify what it is. This could be anything from a lack of skills, knowledge, or resources, to external factors such as competition, market conditions, or personal problems. Understanding the nature of the obstacle is the first step in overcoming it.

2. Develop a Plan: Once you have identified the obstacle, the next step is to develop a plan to overcome it.

This might involve seeking advice or additional resources, developing new skills, or adjusting your approach. The key is to have a clear and actionable plan that will help you overcome the obstacle and achieve your goals.

3.   Seek Support: Overcoming obstacles can be a challenging and lonely journey, and it is important to seek support when needed. This could be from friends, family, or a professional mentor or coach. Having someone to talk to and seek guidance from can be incredibly helpful in overcoming obstacles and dealing with setbacks.

4.   Stay Focused and Positive: Overcoming obstacles requires a positive and focused mindset. It is important to stay focused on your goals and maintain a positive

attitude, even in the face of adversity. Surround yourself with positive influences, avoid negative thoughts and people, and focus on the things that bring you joy and fulfillment.

5.   Learn from Setbacks: Setbacks and failures are inevitable, but it is important to view them as opportunities for growth and learning. Take the time to reflect on your setbacks and understand what you could have done differently. Use this knowledge to develop new strategies and approaches that will help you overcome obstacles in the future.

6.   Celebrate Your Progress: It is important to celebrate your progress and acknowledge the milestones you have achieved along the way. This will help you stay motivated and focused on your goals, even in the face of

obstacles and setbacks. Take time to recognize your achievements, no matter how small, and give yourself credit for the progress you have made.

7.   Stay Resilient: Resilience is the ability to bounce back from setbacks and challenges, and it is an essential part of overcoming obstacles. Stay resilient by focusing on the things that bring you joy and fulfillment, maintaining a positive attitude, and seeking support when needed. By staying resilient, you will be able to overcome obstacles and setbacks and achieve your goals.

Importance of overcoming obstacles:

Overcoming obstacles and dealing with challenges and setbacks is a crucial part of personal and professional growth. No matter what our goals and aspirations may be, we all face obstacles and challenges along the way. However, it is our ability to overcome these challenges and bounce back from setbacks that determine our success and fulfillment in life.

One of the first steps in overcoming an obstacle is to identify what it is. This could be anything from a lack of skills, knowledge, or resources, to external factors such as competition, market conditions, or personal problems. Understanding the nature of the obstacle is essential in overcoming it. Once the obstacle has been identified, the next step is to develop a plan to overcome it. This might involve seeking advice or additional resources, developing new skills, or adjusting our approach. The key is to have a clear and actionable plan that will help us overcome the obstacle and achieve our goals.

Seeking support is an important aspect of overcoming obstacles. Overcoming obstacles can be a challenging and lonely journey, and having someone to talk to and seek guidance from can be incredibly helpful. This could be from friends, family, or a professional mentor or coach. Having a support system can provide us with encouragement and motivation when we need it most.

Having a positive and focused mindset is essential to overcoming obstacles. It is important to stay focused on our goals and maintain a positive attitude, even in the face of adversity. Surrounding ourselves with positive influences, avoiding negative thoughts and people, and focusing on the things that bring us joy and fulfillment can help us stay positive and motivated.

Setbacks and failures are inevitable, but it is important to view them as opportunities for growth and learning. Taking the time to reflect on our setbacks and understand what we could have done differently can help us develop new strategies and approaches that will help us overcome obstacles in the future. Celebrating our progress and acknowledging the milestones we have achieved along the way can help us stay motivated and focused on our goals, even in the face of obstacles and setbacks.

Resilience is the ability to bounce back from setbacks and challenges, and it is an essential part of overcoming obstacles. Staying resilient by focusing on the things that bring us joy and fulfillment, maintaining a positive attitude, and seeking support when needed can help us overcome obstacles and setbacks and achieve our goals. Remember that setbacks and failures are a natural part of the journey to success, and they should not discourage or defeat us. With determination, perseverance, and a positive mindset, we will be able to overcome any obstacle and achieve our dreams.

In conclusion, overcoming obstacles and dealing with challenges and setbacks is a critical aspect of personal and professional development. By identifying the obstacle, developing a plan, seeking support, staying focused and positive, learning from setbacks, celebrating your progress, and staying resilient, you will be able to overcome obstacles and achieve your goals. Remember that setbacks and failures are a natural part of the journey to success, and they should not discourage or defeat you. With determination, perseverance, and a positive mindset, you will be able to overcome any obstacle and achieve your dreams.

CHAPTER TWELVE

Celebrating Success: Reflecting on Your Journey and What's Next

As a business owner or leader, it's important to take the time to celebrate your successes and reflect on the journey that led you to where you are today. Whether your business has hit a major milestone, achieved a significant goal, or simply made it through a challenging year, taking the time to celebrate and reflect can help you to build a stronger, more resilient business that is better equipped to face the future.

Reflecting on Your Journey

One of the most important steps in celebrating success is to reflect on the journey that led you to where you are today. This reflection can help you to understand the challenges and successes that you have experienced, and to gain a deeper appreciation for the hard work and dedication that went into achieving your goals.

As you reflect on your journey, it can be helpful to consider the following questions:

• What were some of the biggest challenges that you faced along the way?

• What were some of the key moments of success or triumph that you experienced?

• What did you learn from these experiences that can help you to be a better business owner or leader in the future?

Answering these questions can help you to gain a clearer understanding of the journey that you have been on, and to identify the key lessons and insights that you have gained along the way.

Celebrating Your Success

Once you have taken the time to reflect on your journey, it's important to celebrate your successes and to recognize the hard work and dedication that went into achieving your goals. This celebration can take many forms, including:

•   Hosting a company-wide celebration or event

•   Providing recognition and rewards to employees

• Sharing your success with stakeholders, including customers, partners, and investors

• Giving back to the community through charitable donations or volunteer work

No matter how you choose to celebrate, the key is to take the time to recognize and appreciate the successes that you have achieved, and to acknowledge the hard work and dedication of everyone who has helped you to get there.

Looking Ahead: What's Next

As you celebrate your successes and reflect on your journey, it's important to also look ahead to the future and consider what's next for your business. This can include:

- Setting new goals and targets for the future

- Developing a strategic plan to help you achieve these goals

- Investing in new technology, processes, or systems that can help you to be more efficient and effective

- Building new partnerships or expanding existing relationships to help you to grow your business

No matter what's next for your business, it's important to have a clear plan in place and to work tirelessly to achieve your goals. By doing so, you can ensure that your business continues to grow and thrive, and that you remain well-positioned to meet the challenges and opportunities of the future.

In conclusion, celebrating success and reflecting on your journey is an important part of building a successful and sustainable business. By taking the time to recognize and appreciate your achievements, to reflect on the journey that led you to where you are today, and to plan for the future, you can ensure that your business remains strong and resilient, and that you are well-equipped to face the challenges and opportunities of the future.

Building a culture of recognition and celebration

In addition to recognizing and celebrating successes at the individual and business level, it's important to also build a culture of recognition and celebration within your organization. This can help to create a positive, motivated, and engaged workforce, and to foster a sense of pride and ownership in the success of the business.

To build a culture of recognition and celebration, you can implement the following strategies:

• Regularly recognizing and celebrating employee achievements and milestones

• Encouraging employees to celebrate their successes with one another

• Providing opportunities for employees to contribute to the success of the business, such as through cross-functional projects or initiatives

• Offering employee development and training programs that help employees to build skills and knowledge, and to take pride in their work

By building a culture of recognition and celebration, you can create a positive and supportive workplace that motivates and engages employees, and that fosters a sense of ownership and pride in the success of the business.

Investing in your people

Another important aspect of celebrating success and building a strong, resilient business is investing in your people. This includes providing employees with the resources and support they need to succeed, and creating opportunities for them to grow and develop both professionally and personally.

To invest in your people, you can implement the following strategies:

•   Offering competitive compensation and benefits packages

•   Providing opportunities for professional development and growth

•   Creating flexible and supportive work environments that meet the needs of employees

•   Encouraging and supporting employees to pursue their passions and interests outside of work.

Investing in your people is an important step in building a successful and sustainable business, and in ensuring that your employees are well-equipped to meet the challenges and opportunities of the future.

Embracing change and growth

Finally, as you celebrate your successes and reflect on your journey, it's important to embrace change and growth, and to be willing to adapt and evolve as your business evolves. This can include:

- Embracing new technology and innovations that can help you to be more efficient and effective

- Adapting to changing market conditions and customer needs

- Encouraging employees to embrace change and to take on new challenges and responsibilities

By embracing change and growth, you can ensure that your business remains relevant and competitive in an ever-changing marketplace, and that you are well-positioned to take advantage of new opportunities and trends.

In conclusion, celebrating success and reflecting on your journey is an important part of building a strong, resilient business. By taking the time to recognize and celebrate your achievements, to invest in your people, and to embrace change and growth, you can ensure that your business remains well-positioned to meet the challenges and opportunities of the future.

Continuing on, it's important to note that reflecting on your journey and celebrating your successes should be an ongoing process, not just a one-time event. Regularly taking the time to assess your progress, celebrate your achievements, and set new goals is essential for ongoing success and growth.

Here are some tips to help you integrate this into your business routine:

• Schedule regular check-ins and progress updates: This can include monthly or quarterly meetings with your team or individual employees to review progress, celebrate successes, and set new goals.

• Encourage open communication: Foster an environment where employees feel comfortable sharing their achievements, successes, and challenges. This can help to build a sense of camaraderie and support, and to ensure that everyone is working towards common goals.

• Celebrate small wins: It's important to celebrate not only major milestones, but also smaller wins and successes along the way. This helps to keep everyone motivated and engaged, and to maintain a positive outlook.

• Recognize the role of failure: Celebrating success also means recognizing the role that failure plays in the journey. Embrace and learn from failure, and use it as an opportunity to grow and improve.

In addition to these tips, there are also many creative ways to celebrate success and recognize achievements, such as hosting team-building events, offering special incentives or rewards, and recognizing employees publicly through company-wide announcements or award ceremonies.

By taking the time to celebrate success and reflect on your journey, you can help to build a positive and motivated workplace, foster a sense of pride and ownership in your business, and ensure that everyone is

working towards common goals.

www.ingramcontent.com/pod-product-compliance
Lightning Source LLC
Chambersburg PA
CBHW071135220526
45467CB00015B/1093